Discovering Maps

Street Maps

Harriet Brundle
and John Willis

AV2
www.openlightbox.com

AV2

Step 1
Go to **www.openlightbox.com**

Step 2
Enter this unique code
CSKXY2YSF

Step 3
Explore your interactive eBook!

AV2 is optimized for use on any device

Your interactive eBook comes with...

Audio — Listen to the entire book read aloud

Videos — Watch informative video clips

Weblinks — Gain additional information for research

Try This! — Complete activities and hands-on experiments

Key Words — Study vocabulary, and complete a matching word activity

Quizzes — Test your knowledge

Slideshows — View images and captions

Share — Share titles within your Learning Management System (LMS) or Library Circulation System

Citation — Create bibliographical references following APA, CMOS, and MLA styles

DISCOVERING MAPS

Street Maps

CONTENTS

What Is a Map?

A map is a picture that gives people information about an **area**. A map could be on paper or it could be digital. Digital maps are on a screen.

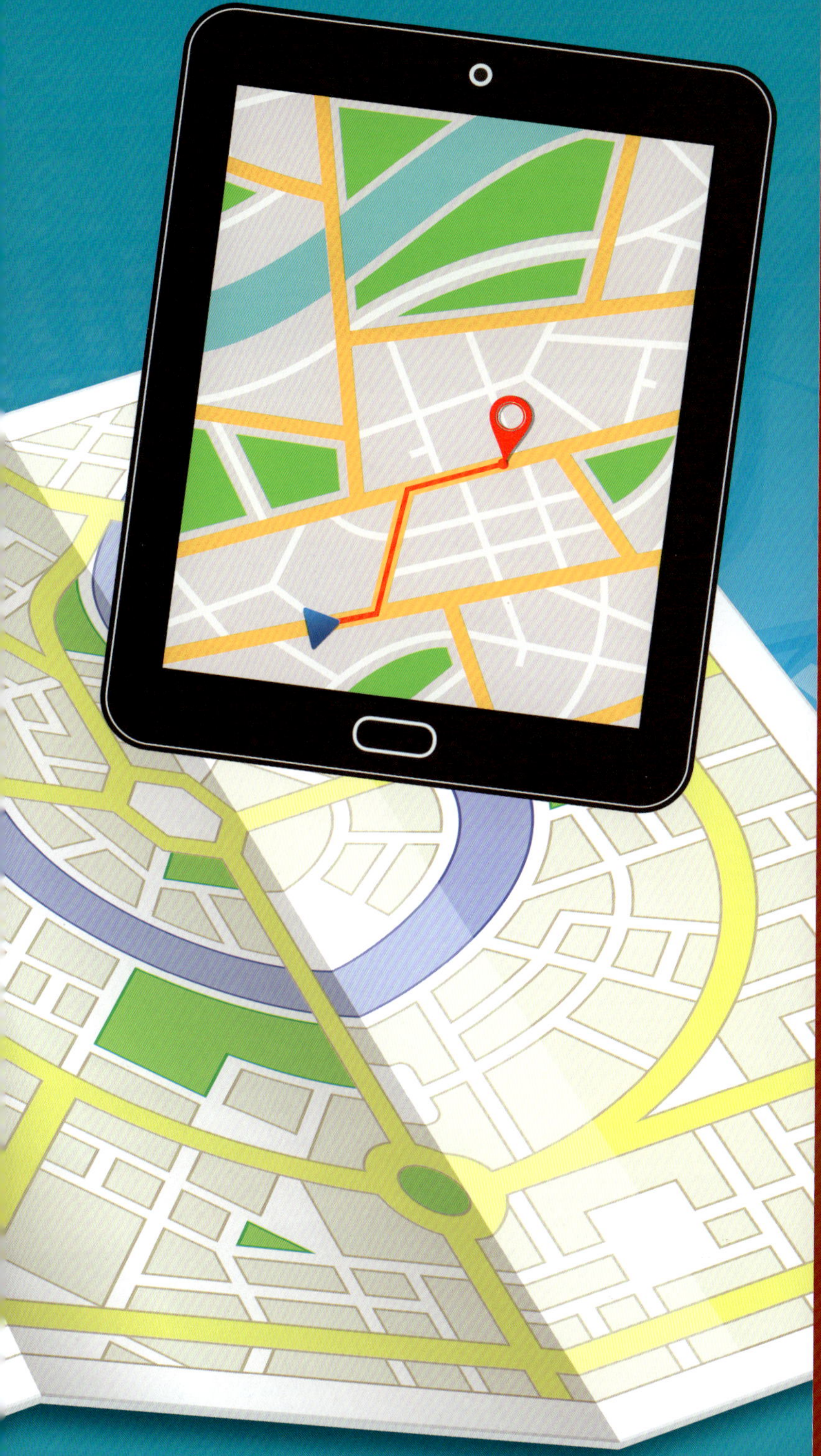

Types of Maps

Country Map

Shows country and state borders.

Physical Map

Shows mountains, rivers, lakes, and other land features.

Street Map

Shows streets, highways, and railways.

Using a Map

Maps have different colors and **symbols** to represent places and buildings.

All maps have a **legend** that explains what the symbols mean.

The color blue is often used on maps to show **bodies of water**.

Map Legend

Often, the symbols on a map look like objects from the places they represent.

Many maps are drawn from a "bird's-eye view." This means that they show how an area looks from above.

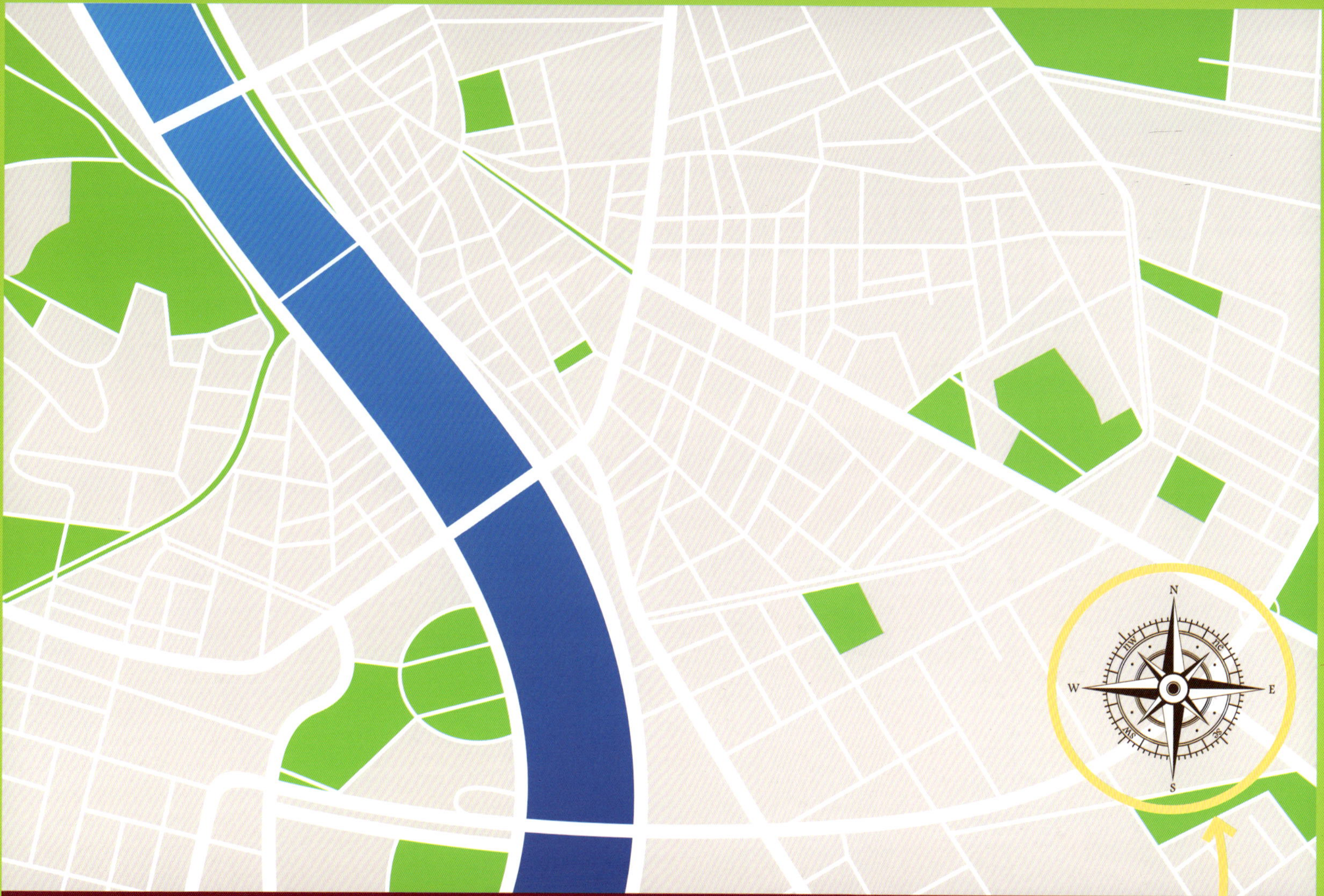

Most maps have a **compass**. It shows which way on the map is north, south, east, or west.

Scale

Everything on a map has been made smaller. The amount by which things have been made smaller is called the scale.

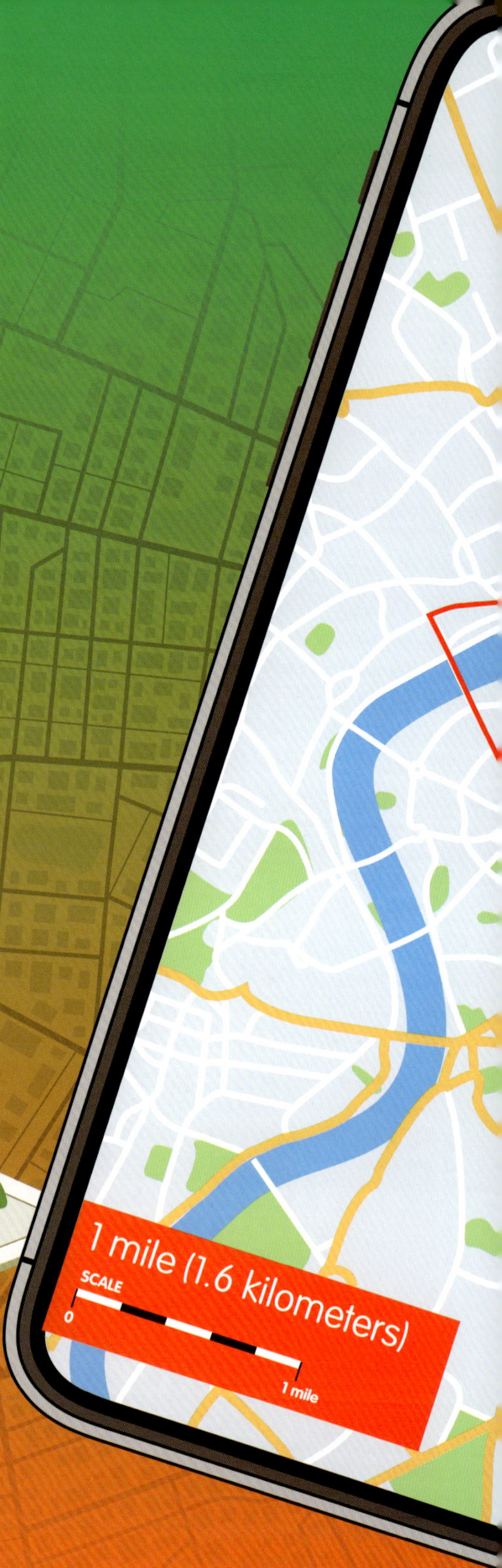

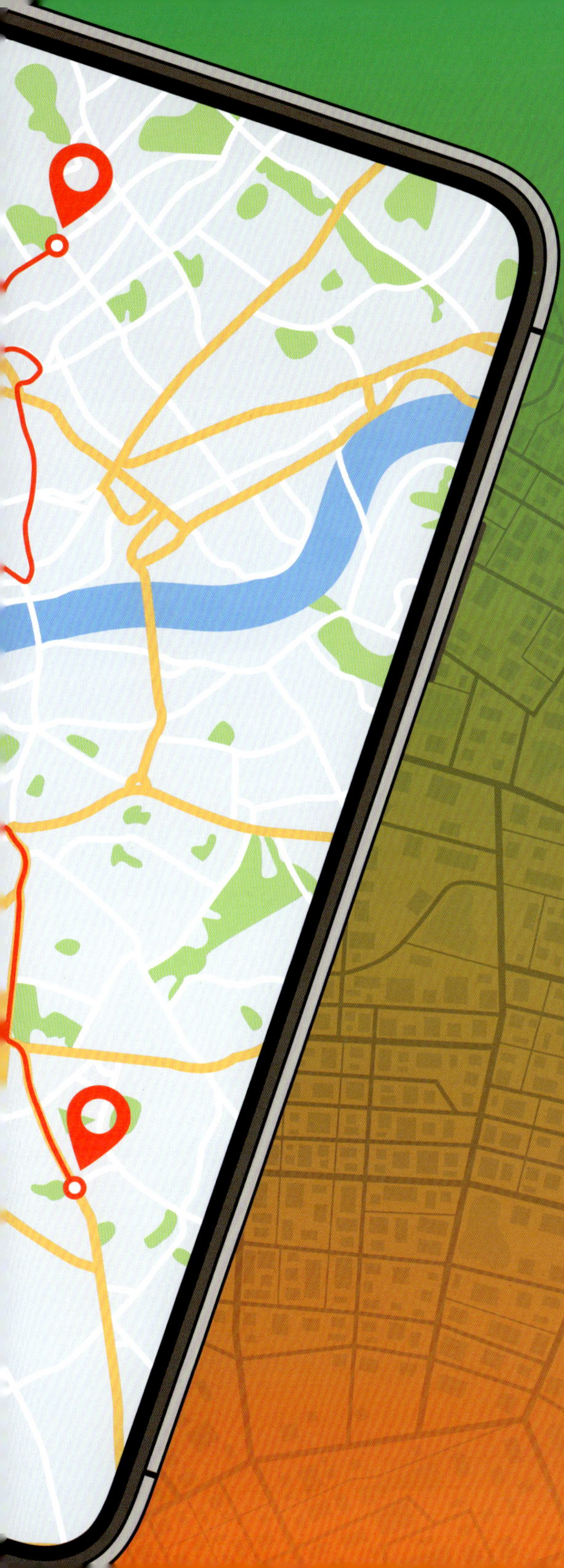

A scale means people can show a long distance on a small map. If someone wants to know how long a road is, they can use the map scale.

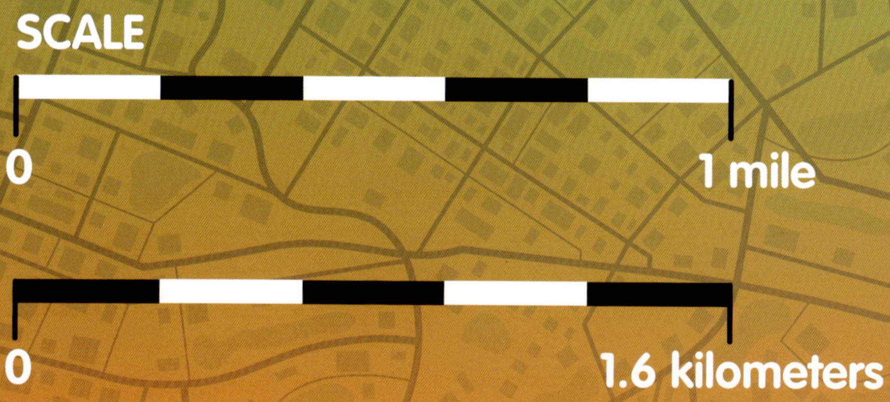

Street Maps

A street map is a map that shows all the different streets in an area.

Some street maps show all the **points of interest** in an area, too.

A street map might also show the different types of **transportation** in that area.

A restaurant is an example of a **point of interest**.

Why Use a Street Map?

People can use a street map to help find the way around their local area.

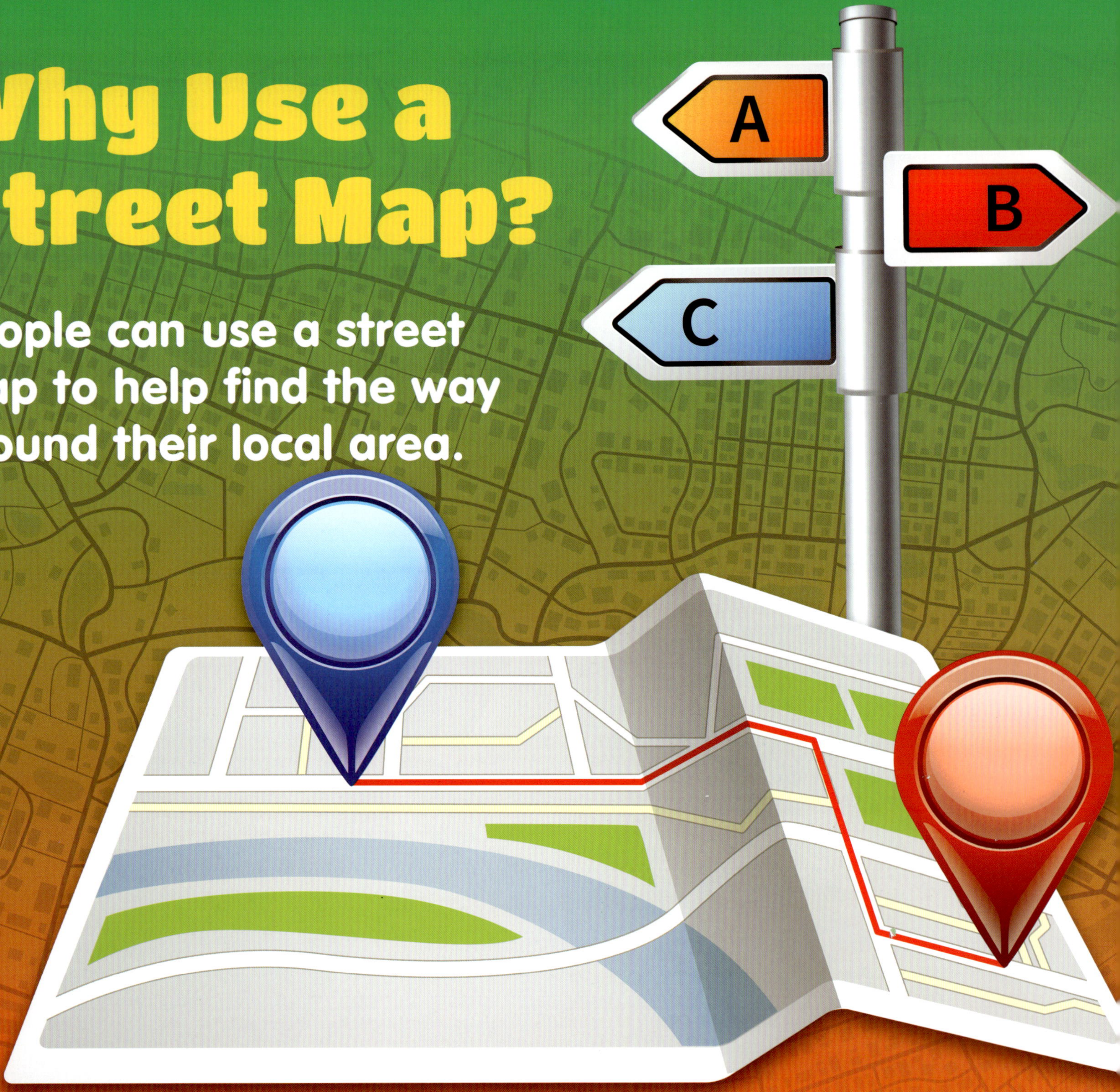

If people want to travel from their house to a nearby park but do not know the way, they can use a street map.

One of the oldest known street maps was created more than 1,600 years ago. It showed roads and points of interest in the Roman Empire.

How Is a Street Map Made?

To make a map, all the important information must be **researched** first. This includes the locations of the points of interest.

You can map your local area. All you need is paper, coloring pens, and a ruler. Take an adult with you and explore your neighborhood.

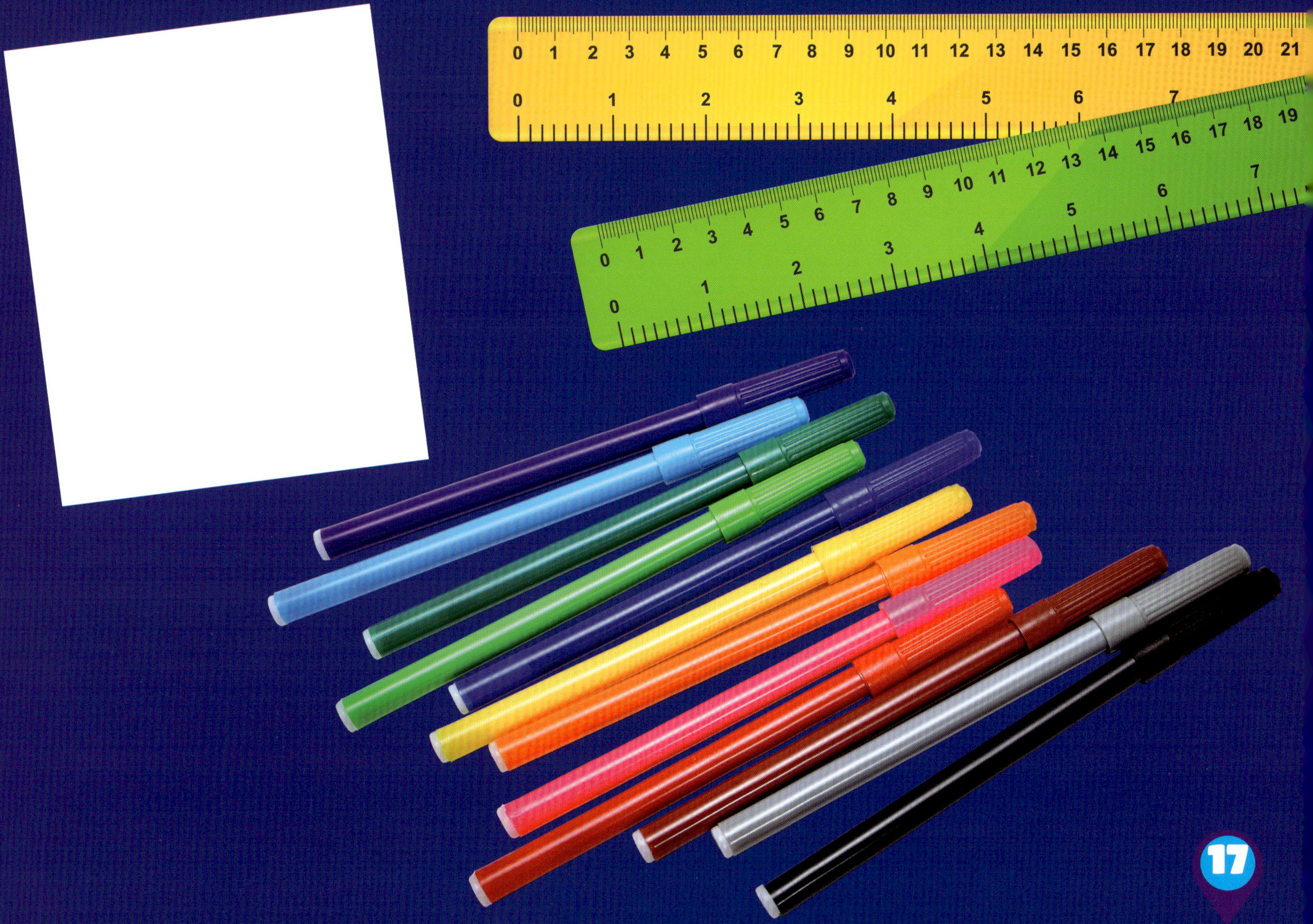

Mapping Your Area

CHOOSE YOUR AREA

Start by thinking about the area you would like to map.

DRAW THE ROADS

Draw the roads in the area you have chosen.

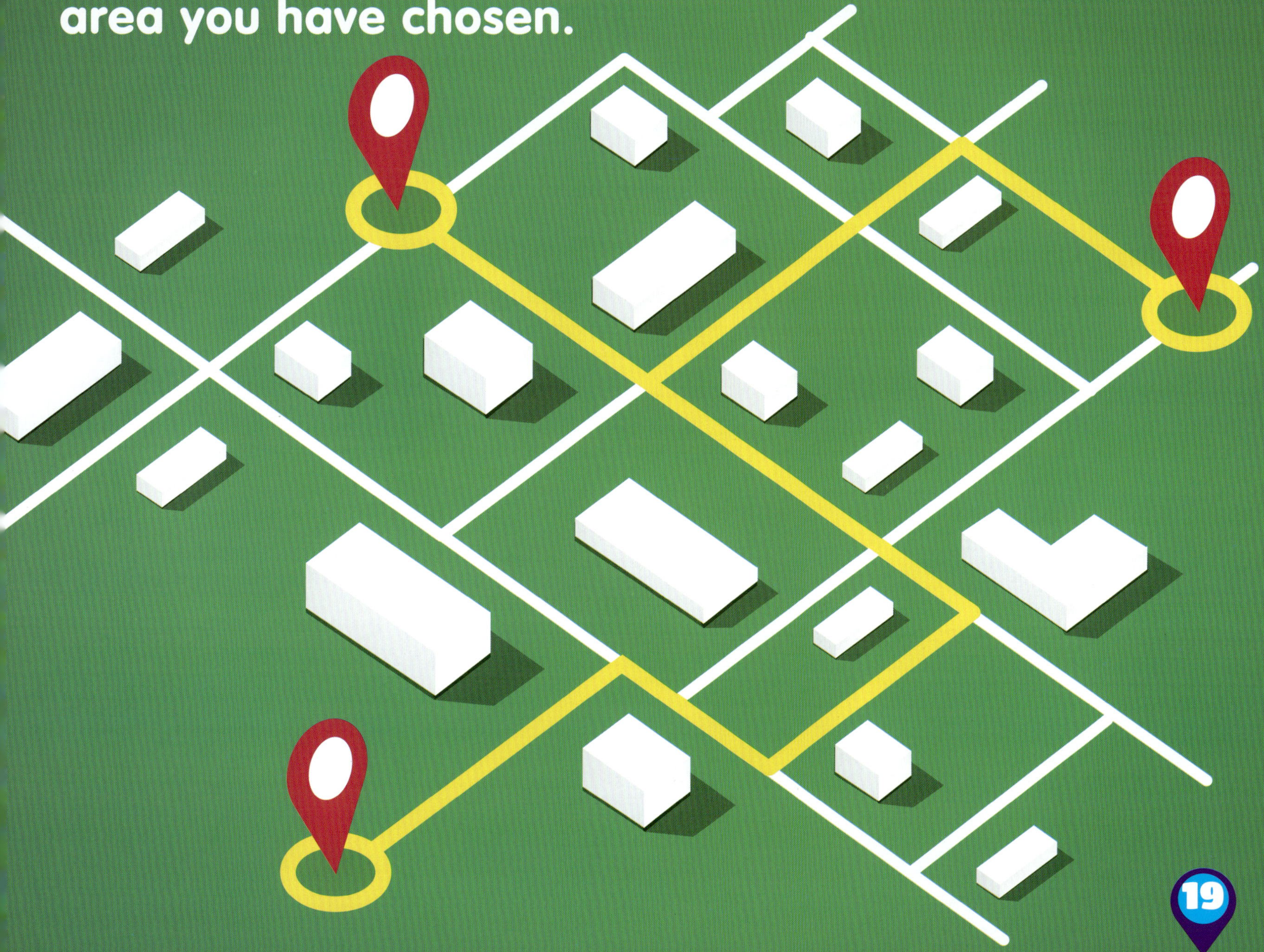

POINTS OF INTEREST

Make a list of any points of interest on your road. Is there a school or a shop nearby?

CREATE A LEGEND

Create symbols for the points of interest. Then, add them to the map in the correct place.

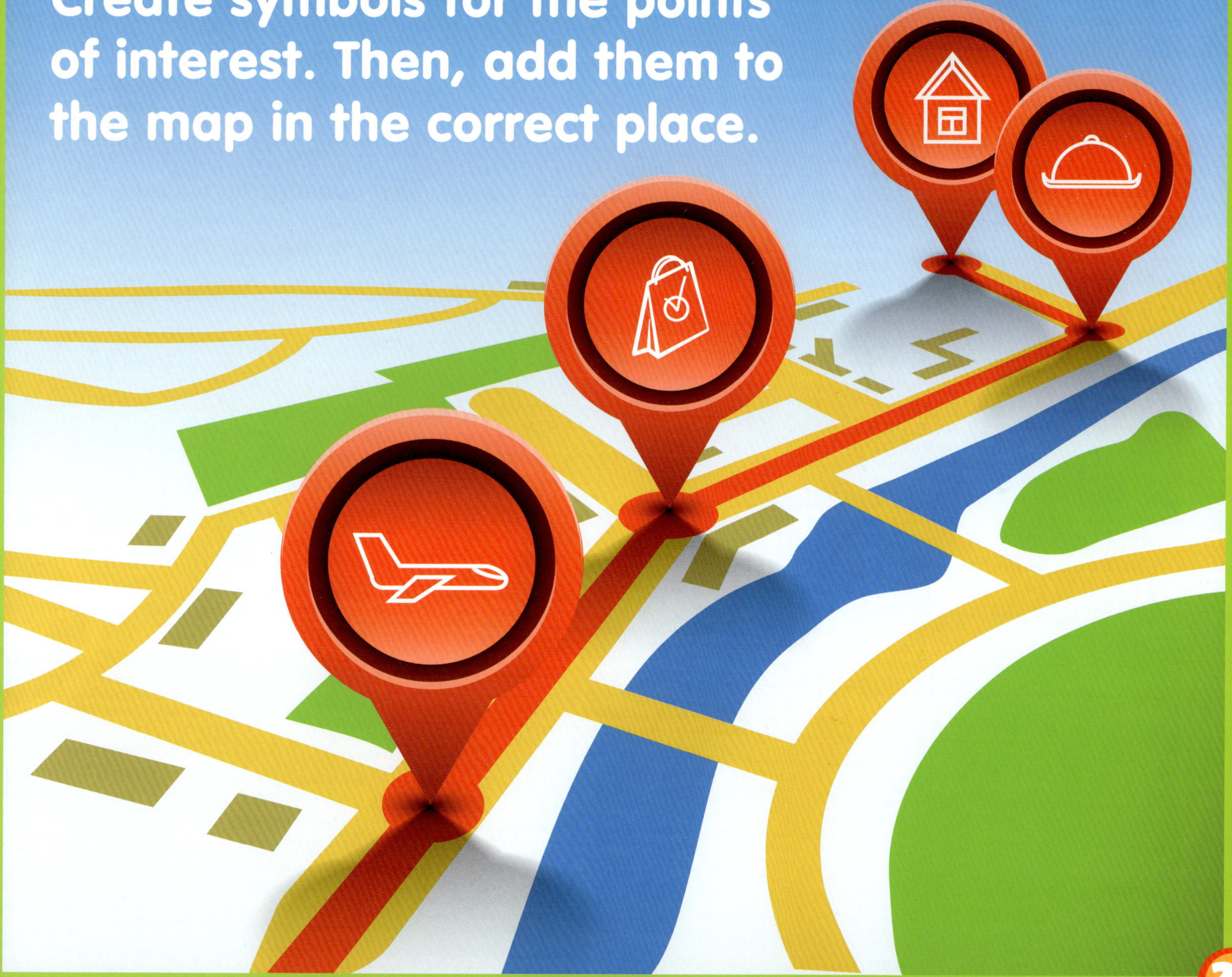

Be Creative!

Create the street map of your dream location. Would you love to live next-door to a movie theater, or have a zoo in your garden?

Draw the roads in your dream location. Then, add all the points of interest to complete your map.

ZOO

KEY WORDS

Research has shown that as much as 65 percent of all written material published in English is made up of 300 words. These 300 words cannot be taught using pictures or learned by sounding them out. They must be recognized by sight. This book contains 98 common sight words to help young readers improve their reading fluency and comprehension. This book also teaches young readers several important content words, such as proper nouns.

Page	Sight Words First Appearance
4	a, about, an, are, be, could, gives, is, it, on, or, paper, people, picture, that, what
5	and, country, land, mountains, of, other, rivers, shows, state
6	all, different, have, mean, often, places, the, to, water
7	from, like, look, they
8	above, eye, how, many, this
9	most, way, which
10	been, by, has, made, mile, things
11	can, if, know, long, small, use, wants
12	also, in, might, points, too
13	example
14	around, find, help, their, why
15	but, do, house, more, not, one, than, was, years
16	first, important, make, must
17	need, take, with, you, your
18	start, would
20	any, list, school, there
21	add, for, them, then

Page	Content Words First Appearance
4	area, information, map, screen
5	borders, features, highways, lakes, railways, streets
6	bodies, buildings, colors, legend, symbols
7	airport, gasoline station, objects, restaurant
8	view
9	compass
10	scale
11	distance
12	streets, transportation
15	park, Roman Empire
17	adult, coloring pens, neighborhood, ruler
20	shop

Published by Lightbox Learning Inc.
276 5th Avenue, Suite 704 #917
New York, NY 10001
Website: www.openlightbox.com

Library of Congress Control Number available upon request.

ISBN 978-1-5105-6362-9 (hardcover)
ISBN 979-8-8745-1508-9 (softcover)
ISBN 978-1-5105-6364-3 (static multi-user eBook)
ISBN 978-1-5105-8147-0 (interactive multi-user eBook)

Printed in Guangzhou, China
1 2 3 4 5 6 7 8 9 0 28 27 26 25 24

052024
100923

Project Coordinator: John Willis
Designer: Jean Faye Rodriguez

The publisher acknowledges Getty Images and Shutterstock as the primary image suppliers for this title.

First published by BookLife in 2018